Author: © 2011 E. Carolina Quevedo

info@elisequevedo.com

Cover Design: Faye McGovern & Ultraviolet Designs
Assisted by: Debi Kieserman

Publisher: CreateSpace, a DBA of On-Demand Publishing, LLC

2nd Edition August 2011
1st Edition March 2011

Dedicated to my mom Rosario.

CONTENTS

E. Carolina Quevedo

ACKNOWLEDGEMENTS

A special thank-you goes to:

My mom, Rosario: We may have been apart for many years, and we may have lived in different countries for over a decade, but you have always been there for me. You always said I could be anything I wanted to be. Mom, this book is for you, so you can be proud of your daughter. You brought me up on your own and sacrificed everything to give me the best life you possibly could. I love you very much.

Lisa J.: Coach, mentor, and friend, you were the one who started it all! You showed me what being a woman of power is all about. You taught me that anything is possible and raised my confidence. You truly are a great inspiration to every woman and princess on earth and I will always thank God for bringing our paths together. I have so much to thank you for. Love ya girl!

Jacquie C.: Hey, sis! You truly are a woman of success. Your accomplishments speak for themselves. Your stage presence is unforgettable, and I can't wait to be on stage with you again. You've made dreams of mine come true and it will never be forgotten. You have the Kick-Ass Attitude this book is all about. Love ya!

Alan L.: My adoptive mentor. What can I say? I wouldn't be here today if it weren't for your belief and encouraging words. You showed me what having passion for what you believe in is all about. Hats off to you and your lovely wife, Carol, for the incredible legacy and empire you guys have created. Big hug!! Love you both!

Michael M.: One of my business partners whom I respect a lot. You taught me perseverance always pays off. You have a great attitude both in life and business; you're always trying to better yourself. I thank you for always believing in me. Always in my heart!

Rodney D.: Known to me as the master communicator. I have learned so much from you, and your hospitality in San Diego, CA will never be forgotten. Your charismatic persona is contagious, and your integrity and values are beyond anything I have ever seen. I will see you in Del Mar for a round of golf very soon. Lots of luv!

Alex H-B : Friend and partner in crime. You've inspired me and told me off when needed! Thank you for believing in our projects and always striving to do better. Always be proud. You are an amazing human being and I'm very grateful to have you in my life. Love ya!

And I can't forget my Quantum Leap Coaching and cruise partners: Debi, Dan, Joseph, Robyn, Troy, Julie, Lilija, Cherill, Robin, and Karen. You are all amazing and have the Kick-Ass Attitude that got us all together!

And my UK family away from home family: Amanda, Lee, Jordan,

Tom and Kieran! You are my second family and are always in my heart.

And finally, to **Shawn D.** , someone who saw something in me. You believed in me first when others thought I wouldn't make it,

showed me what leadership is all about and gave me my first opportunity to be a leader and train others. That will never be forgotten. You are a great inspiration,. Lots of luv.

Be true to yourself, be honest, and never lose integrity.

Treat others the way you want to be treated.

Never stop believing.

And foremost,

CREATE A KICK-ASS ATTITUDE!!!!!!

Love you all

INTRODUCTION

Hey there! I'm very excited to share this book with all of you. Every story shared, every word, every sentence comes from the heart. This book is dedicated to everyone who has believed in me and pushed me to be the best I possibly can be.

If I can inspire anyone to smile, be better in life, or create a Kick-Ass Attitude, my job is done. I turned my life around thanks to personal development, and this book is the start of my giving back what I have learned.

I wrote *Creating a Kick Ass Attitude* to help anyone who has ever had doubts about achieving something or doesn't believe they can do better in life. It is to inspire people to make the most out of any situation.

There's no better time than now to create a positive attitude to achieve your goals and dreams. Attitude, bonding, conviction, integrity, and passion are what I'm all about. I want to help you discover a new world, discover a new you.

Attitude is the starting point for any task we wish to accomplish, and it is the first part in the equation of success. You may have the best Kick-Ass Attitude in life, but if you don't combine it with hard work, sweat, determination, and dedication, success will knock on someone else's door. What I want from everyone who reads this book is to simply smile at the end and realize, "We can all be success stories."

I have come across so many negative people, and I want everyone to realize that success begins with your attitude! I've also seen a few friends change and lose their sense of who they truly are. The best thing you can do in life is to be true to yourself. Don't change to please others, and remember who your friends are. As Joseph Sugarman said, "Each time you are honest and conduct yourself with honesty, a success force will drive you toward greater success. Each time you lie, even with a little white lie, there are strong forces pushing you toward failure."

Attitude is everything in life.

Make today the day that changes the rest of your life.

Love to all,

Elise Quevedo

1

SOMETIMES IT'S GOOD TO THINK LIKE A CHILD

Have you ever wondered why so many people never follow their dreams? Have you ever looked around you when you are on the bus, waiting in line at the bank or grocery store, or even just around in the street?

When you were a kid, you had dreams . . . you wanted to be a firefighter, an actor, a pilot, a billionaire, Spider-Man!!! There were no limits to what you wanted to become.

THE COOKIE JAR

Remember that jar of cookies on top of the refrigerator? The jar that you couldn't reach? And do you remember doing everything you could to reach that jar? I still remember thinking, "I want that cookie no matter what." I remember grabbing a chair, and then some books, and stacking them all up, one on top of the other, until I could climb up all the way and get the cookie. I didn't think about the difficulties or how high the books were getting as I stacked them up.

As a child, the notion of fear is non-existent, and we think anything we want is achievable. What happens to our dreams, as we grow old? So many people around us say "NO" that we get used to it, and we let that word affect the way we think.

Why is it that the little boy who wanted to be a firefighter ends up being an accountant? Or the little girl who wanted to be a ballerina ends up being a schoolteacher? We let the people around us influence our decisions. We forget our goals and follow what we think everyone else wants from us.

Each of us must write out our goals and dreams and have them near us each day. If you don't have a goal or plan of where you want to go in life, you will usually not like where you end up.

What you have done up until now—up until ten seconds ago—is GONE! You can't change it! But you can change what you do as of now—this minute, this second.

Lao Tzu once said, "When I let go of what I am, I become what I might be." Let go of the past. Think of whom you want to become and don't let other people tell you otherwise. Keep your focus and remember how driven and courageous you were as a kid. Never forget that feeling.

THE NET CLIMBER

I was talking to a friend recently and was asking him what he had been up to the previous the weekend. About a week prior to this conversation, I had given him a great book called *Conquer Fear* by Lisa Jimenez, one of my mentors.

My friend says, "I have a great story for you Elise!" And the story went something like this . . . . My friend has a four-year-old daughter, and like any parent, he is very protective of her. They were at the park and his daughter was about to climb a very high net climber. He immediately ran to her to stop her and say, "NO! Don't go up there! It's too dangerous!

But then, just as he was about to talk to her, he remembered what he had learned while reading the book, and instead of telling her no; he changed it to, "Be careful as you climb. Watch your step, OK? I'll be right here." She climbed up and nothing happened. She was safe, she was happy, and there was no danger.

So what's the moral of the story? A child doesn't see difficulties as adults do. Children think with a much more positive attitude! Why did my friend run up to his daughter when she was going to climb the net climber? Because as adults, we see the difficulties first. We go into panic mode without reason for the tiniest things in life. His daughter didn't see that. She just saw this fun climber and wanted to go on it. It wasn't a difficulty; it was a fun challenge.

Wouldn't it be great to sometimes think like a child when we are dealing with daily challenges? People like me, entrepreneurs, we fall flat on the floor a lot of times! But guess what—we get up again! I always tell people I'm like a bouncy punching bag. You know the one I'm talking about. You can punch it as hard as you want, but it always bounces back up. It's always thinking positive!

That's the way I like to see life. Some people see the glass half empty, and others see it half full, but I see it FULL! Half full of water—and half full of air!

It all comes down to our way of thinking, and we can all learn to think more positively. Like I said, you can't change what you did ten minutes ago, one minute ago, or ten seconds ago. But you CAN change what you do and how you think as of today, as of right now, this minute—and this second.

Think more like a child each day! And I don't mean act childish. There's a huge difference. Take the part of the child that has no fear! The part that sees everything as a fun challenge. How many times did you fall off your bicycle when you were learning to ride it? Quite a few, I presume. And did that stop you from getting on it again and again until you were able to ride it alone? Of course not!

How many times as a kid did you cry because you hurt yourself when you were learning how to use your Rollerblades? And how long did that cry last? Fifteen seconds? Twenty seconds? Within five minutes, you had a bandage on and were trying again! When you were learning to walk, how many times did you attempt to get up after a fall? Thousands! You didn't stop trying because you couldn't walk the first time!

The bottom line is, from the time we're babies we come across challenges, but as we get older, we change the way we think and react to those challenges.

Make today the day that changes the rest of your life. Make today the day that you take control of your life, your business, your relationship, your faith . . . anything you want! Write those goals down and start living again with a better attitude!

Inside every child's imagination lies the possibility to be anyone they want to be. So you aren't a kid anymore; that shouldn't stop you from having the same imagination. Find the people around you who think like you, and surround yourself with a team of individuals who will stop at nothing until they reach their goals.

Some people will read the title of this chapter and automatically say this book is wrong, that children are children and adults are adults. That you can't think like a child at all! But I suppose that's what having freedom of speech and an opinion is all about.

DISNEYLAND STORY

Let me share a fun fact about myself. Can you believe I've been to Disneyland Paris eleven times? I've also gone to Walt Disney World in Orlando and the original Disneyland in Anaheim twice each!

That is quite a few times, considering my first visit was about eight years ago. That's an average of two trips a year to a Disney theme park. I'm a big kid at heart, but most importantly, it's a place where dreams are kept alive. Call it a fantasyland or a kids' world, but to this day, many adults go there without children and many weddings are celebrated on their grounds.

Have you noticed people visiting Disneyland are always happy? Smiling? It always seems to bring you back to when you were a kid. That's probably why I love it so much. About a month ago, I took one of my friends to Disneyland Paris, as she is twenty-eight and had never been there. I couldn't believe it! So we drove the six hours from the UK to Disneyland just for the day. We had a blast! We ran around like children, getting on as many rides as we could; we had lunch at the Lucky Nugget, where you can meet Disney characters, and we didn't stop smiling all day!

My friend slept the whole way back, just like a kid, while I drove. It doesn't matter how old we are, Disney will always have a place in our hearts, because it's a place of happiness, dreams, and laughter.

Why am I sharing this with you? Because this is one of my happy places, one of the places that reminds me that when I was a kid, I wanted to do everything. Just like when you go to a Disney park, you want to get on every ride, you want to meet every character, and anything is possible!

How many times have you heard people say, "Think of a happy place," when things are not going right or when you are stressed? Thinking like a child is just like that. Going back to a happy place where anything is possible. Where everyone around you thinks like you. So create that happy place and visit it once in a while. You don't have to physically go there, just mentally. Our brains are more powerful than we give them credit for.

To finish this chapter, I'd like to leave you with a great quote by Ralph Waldo Emerson:

To speak truly, few adult persons can see nature. Most persons do not see the sun. At least they have a very superficial seeing. The sun illuminates only the eye of the man, but shines into the eye and heart of the child. The lover of nature is he whose inward and outward senses are still truly adjusted to each other; who has retained the spirit of infancy even into the era of manhood.

2

YOUR JOB ATTITUDE

MONDAY BLUES

Who can forget those Monday blues? Most of us have suffered from those days when we don't want to go to work.

What is it about Monday mornings? For most people, especially office workers (or nine-to-fivers, as I like to call them), Monday morning is like a duel. It is their nemesis, a fearful day, a day you dread after a nice relaxing weekend.

A couple of days ago, I was having dinner and catching up with one of my oldest friends. She had just come back after visiting her family for the holidays and had a great time. But one of the first things she said was, "I'm back to work on Monday. I don't want to go back; I have so much work to catch up on."

Have you ever noticed most conversations on a Monday start like this? "I had such a great weekend, BUT now it's back to reality." Or, "I so needed that vacation, BUT I did not want to come back."

That's what a lot of people hear most Mondays. We also hear, "The weather is horrible today," "Still five days to go before the weekend," "I don't feel like working today."

So many people are unhappy with their current job, and they will be for the rest of their lives. How different would it be if you learned to change the attitude you have toward your job?

If you're reading this book and you're in a job that you don't like, then congratulations! You are taking the first step toward changing your attitude and discovering personal development. And if, like me, you are doing what you love and are still on that journey of self-discovery, then congratulations too! Because you can join me on the journey and teach others what attitude can do.

NINE-TO-FIVERS

A few years back, I was doing office work as a nine-to-fiver. Throughout the day I would hear people say all those negative things, and I decided I wouldn't let them change the way I thought or behaved. I challenged myself to say, "I am fantastic! How are you today?" every time someone said, "Good day, how are you today?" After a few weeks of saying that, people would come up to me and say, "Good day, fantastic! How are you today?" And I would answer, "You said it! I am FANTASTIC! What else would I be?!"

Imagine going to work and hearing negative words every minute, every hour, every day, five days a week, four weeks a month, twelve months a year! Can you imagine what that does to your attitude toward work?

Even as a positive person, it's hard to keep an upbeat conversation or thought when everyone around you is negative, right? Wrong! Through mental toughness, a positive attitude, and personal development, you can help change the way you think and change the way those around you behave. It's not an easy task, but it sure is a fun challenge and one that I am always up for. It does require patience, but the rewards are priceless.

It's not important where you're at right now; it's where you can be in the future that matters. Give 100% effort every day at your job. If you're going to do something, you might as well do it right. The job you have right now pays for your rent, gas for the car, your food, and your clothes.

No matter what your job is right now, it is your attitude that will keep you going when everything seems to be going wrong or everyone around you is throwing you negative energy.

BEING GRATEFUL

Be grateful that you have a job! A lot of people out there don't have a job or a home. We like to complain about things we have control over. But for a minute, picture this: hunger, no home, no clean water to drink, no clothes to change into, no movie theatre, no malls, no luxuries.

Are you a little bit more grateful now? We get so accustomed to what we have that we forget how to appreciate what is around us. Even if you don't like your job right now or you're on the path to rediscovery or are simply taking a break in your life, be thankful that you have a roof over your head, food on your plate, and clothes on your body every day.

When you learn how to appreciate life more, you will start to change the way you think and, in turn, your attitude toward your job. For many years I worked jobs I knew were not my dream jobs, but I always knew they were part of my journey and not my destination.

Everything we do in life is part of the journey. You need to set your goals and know what your dreams are and know that everything you do in life will be a learning and growing experience. Every failure, every turn, every fall, every challenge we go through in life is an opportunity to develop ourselves into what we will become as we get older and wiser.

The learning chapter in our lives will never close until we take the last breath on this earth, for learning is an ongoing experience. But it all starts with our attitude.

Change your attitude, change your thoughts.

Change your thoughts, change your actions.

Change your actions, change your results.

Tomorrow, when you get out of bed, smile. And when you go to work, smile. And wish everyone a good day! Don't let people affect the way you think and the way your day is going to be. Make every day a great day at work. Smiling is contagious—if you keep it up, you'll see people smiling back.

Think of it as a challenge if you want, but have fun with it! Don't let other people's thoughts clutter your mind and bring you down. Instead, be confident, give positive vibes and smiles, and see what comes your way.

It's really hard to be negative around someone who is smiling all the time. Sometimes people need to let it out and moan, and that's OK. But don't let them go on for the whole day! If someone is angry, be a good listener, sit down with them, listen to them, let them get it out of their system, ask them if they feel better, and then tell them the rest of their day is going to be a great day!

The reason people go on and on all day is that they keep getting ammunition back. It's like a battle. If you keep shooting at the enemy, they keep shooting back, right? But if you don't shoot, they stop too, because they don't know what you're going to do next.

In a conversation, if someone throws negative comments at you (e.g., the weather is horrible, it's Monday again, it's so cloudy, it's too cold, it's too hot, etc.) and you answer back, the conversation will keep going from bad to worse for the rest of the day. But if you don't throw back similar words, the other person will stop. Instead, try hitting back with positive comments throughout the day.

I remember last year, the mailman said to me, "It's a pleasure delivering the mail to this unit, just to see your smile." I was surprised, and I asked him what he meant. He said that every day, he would deliver mail to hundreds of places and everyone was miserable, but every time he saw me, I would smile and ask him how his day was. He said I was always happy.

I replied, "It all comes down to the way you look at life. I'd rather smile than frown. Why be sad and miserable? We only have one life, and I choose to have a positive attitude every day. If I can make one more person smile each day, my job is done." And of course, the mailman left with a smile.

Smiling doesn't cost you any money. Trying your best at what you do doesn't cost you any money. But being miserable and complaining too much can cost you money! People will get bored of that attitude and they'll hire someone with a better one.

People are influenced by what you do and say. Napoleon Hill once said, "Think twice before you speak, because your words and influence will plant the seed of either success or failure in the mind of another." He was so right. We tend to speak without thinking, and we don't always realize the effect our words have on other people. We also don't understand how much influence our workplace has on our lives. We drag our problems home, and we talk about it with our friends when we go out.

What puzzles me is that people listen to the negative comments more than they listen to the positive ones. I've listened to work conversations that go on forever, and they are all about what he said or she said, but never in a positive manner. For example:

"He had such a bad attitude when he came in that he ruined my day."

"She was cursing so much that everyone's morale was down for the rest of the day."

"He is never happy with what we do; he always looks at the negative side of things."

"She never praises anyone for their hard work; it's never good enough."

And the list could keep on going. Those are examples of conversation starters I've heard when someone asks, "How was work today?" Then it leads to a huge conversation concentrating on the negative side of work. It seems to get the ball rolling. Anyone who has read *Law of Attraction* by Michael Losier knows that negative thoughts bring on negative vibes, ruining your day!

I'm sure in every workplace there is at least one person with a great attitude and positive energy flow, but they tend to be overshadowed by the other 99%, the negative people. It seems to be much easier to talk about what 99% of people do and say than what 1% does and says.

SEMINARS

Corporations come across low morale among their employees all the time, and CEOs often hire corporate and motivational speakers to conduct workshops to boost morale. Even though this is a great idea in theory, employees don't seem to really grasp the concept. And if they do, they quickly forget.

Not long ago, a lawyer friend of mine attended a two-day mandatory seminar at his company. They wanted to boost their team's spirit and get them all motivated to work harder and be happier at work. For two days, I got these awesome calls from my friend. He loved the seminar, the speaker, and all the positive mental attitude he was gaining. I could hardly get a word in, and it was great! I was so proud of him, as he had been a bit down due to a case he was working on. Everyone in the office was being negative because they were working very long hours and weren't getting enough rest.

For a week following the seminar, my friend was so full of energy. He wanted to apply everything he had learned, and he was ready to treat people differently. But soon after, he was back to where he was before attending the seminar. He was influenced by the people around him, who also enjoyed the seminar, but weren't applying what they had learned. As he was spending so much time with the people at work, he let their negative energy influence his thoughts and actions.

I have seen this after many seminars. People attend these great conventions; listen to speakers, and buy books, thinking they are magic wands that will change their lives overnight. But it doesn't work like that.

Being more positive, having a better attitude, creating success, and being who you want to be in life is not an overnight crusade. It has to be applied every day. But people don't apply it—we listen to the people around us who are in the same place as we are, instead of following the advice of those who are successful and have already made it.

Take charge of your attitude at work. Start listening to the ones who have gone a step further if you want to advance in your career. Having a Kick-Ass Attitude at work is about being a leader, filtering the thoughts that stay in our minds when we are at work, and not letting anyone bring us down.

As Francesca Reigler once said, "Happiness is an attitude. We either make ourselves miserable or happy and strong. The amount of work is the same."

So be happy at your workplace. Don't let anyone ruin your happiness. It is your attitude toward your job that will get you through the day. Take one day at the time and kick ass at what you do!

3

RELATIONSHIPS—WE CAN ALL GET BETTER

He likes me, he likes me not. Why hasn't he called? He never listens! He didn't notice my hair! Ladies, recognize any of that?

She's always on the phone! She needs to lighten up! Why does she want me to go shopping with her again? What is it with the clothes coordination? She's always complaining! Gentleman, recognize those words?

Whether you're a man or a woman, this chapter may bring some enlightenment toward the attitude you have in relationships. And not just when it comes to love, but to all of your relationships.

JUST FOR THE LADIES

For now, let's talk about the ladies, my fellow sisters. And don't worry, guys. I'll talk to you shortly.

Now ladies, how many nights have we spent crying because he said he was going to call but he didn't? How many times have we looked for the perfect outfit to wear to dinner just to have him to cancel at the last minute, leaving us enraged? How many times have we looked at our watch while waiting for him when he's late again! How many fights have we had because he wanted to watch the game and we wanted him to spend time with us watching a romantic movie?

Ladies, stop! Most men were not born to go clothes shopping, rent romantic movies, notice our hair, or call at the exact time they said they were going to call. It is a learning process.

If we spent more time enjoying each other and valuing each other's strengths, there would be a lot less fighting between couples. It all comes down to the attitude we have when looking at each situation. In our heads, we want a Prince Charming, with the looks of George Clooney, the body of James Bond, and the thoughtfulness and passion you find in *Romeo and Juliet* or a romance novel. Wait; maybe I'm just describing what I wanted. Ha!

Well, ladies, snap out of it! Even though there are a few people in the world who may possess all those qualities, most of us are not perfect and are a work in progress. We try so hard to change the men we are with that we don't let them be who they are and help them develop their strengths. There's a big difference between trying to change a man physically (remember physical appearance changes as we get older anyway) and helping our partner become a better person spiritually and intellectually.

We concentrate on the little things that won't matter a year from today. There's a brilliant book by Richard Carlson that covers all these little things called, *Don't Sweat the Small Stuff . . . and It's All Small Stuff*, which I recommend to everyone.

A lot of women might read this and think, "Well, I want the best—I won't settle for second best nor do I want to work on changing anyone." The reality is that we miss opportunities when they come knocking because we have the wrong attitude. "He's too short, he's too tall, he's bald, he's too hairy, he doesn't have any muscles, he has too many muscles, he doesn't have a job, he works too many hours."

Do you see how silly it is to concentrate on what doesn't really matter? We are so worried about finding Mr. Right, who we think possesses all the qualities we want that we may have already missed out on someone great.

Remember, everyone can change. What if you met someone who had six out of the ten qualities you want in a man, but after talking to him you realized he was working on the other four? Would you give him a chance? Or would you not even look at him because he wasn't the perfect 10?

I'm not saying you have to say yes to everyone. Simply be more open to what's around you. Communication is the key when finding the perfect companion to spend the rest of your life with. That's what dating is for—to go out with someone a few times and figure out all those things you have in common and the things you are doing to make yourself into a better person. Maybe you are already there and are willing to guide someone else or let yourself be guided.

So, ladies, stop sobbing if you are single. Celebrate being single! You are a woman of power and this is your time to do the things you want to do in life. And if you have someone special in your life, then celebrate that too!

It all comes down to attitude. Forget the past; don't let it determine your thoughts. Start today with a new attitude, and you will attract whatever it is you want.

AND NOW FOR THE GUYS

So guys, remember those complaints? She's always on the phone! She needs to lighten up! Why does she want me to go shopping with her? What is it with the clothes coordination? She's always complaining! Blah, blah, blah.

You should know by now that most women enjoy going shopping, renting romantic movies, getting their hair done, and calling you at the exact time they said they were going to call.

Learning what women want is not an easy task and it never will be! So get used to it, guys. Women are complex individuals—but admit it, you can't live without them.

As I'm on the other side, I don't want to come down too harshly on you. I'll, simply give you a bit of advice regarding your attitude, and maybe by just changing the way you do certain things; you can improve your relationships.

All the things mentioned at the beginning, like noticing a woman's new hairdo or clothes, remembering an anniversary, going to a romantic movie, or having a picnic, just to name a few, aren't there to make your life difficult. Women would simply like to be noticed once in a while, to be taken out and treated like princesses!

So, would it be so hard to do something special for your partner, maybe once a week? Probably not.

There are lots of you out there who already do all those things and more and treat your other half in a very special way. Some people are great at remembering birthdays and dates that are important, and some people aren't. So for the people who easily forget those important dates, couldn't you just write them down on your calendar or keep them on your Blackberry? You never forget when the Super Bowl is. How about making that kind of an effort for your other half?

Honesty is key when being with someone. No two women are alike, which most of you know very well. So ask your partner what things are important to her, then write them down. For example, for me, my birthday is just like any other day. I don't see it as a big deal, so a small intimate dinner or a day out is enough. I don't need a big party or fuss. But I do make a fuss about an anniversary or events involving my business life, so I would expect my partner to make notes on those dates and do something nice for me. I am quite open, so I would tell my partner what's important and what's not. You guys are not psychic, so without us telling you what we consider important, how can we expect anything special to be done?

The key is communication. When entering a new relationship, get to know that person, what she likes, what's important to her. Remember, it's not about shouting from the rooftop each day that you love someone; it's about each day's interaction with each other and small thoughtful actions.

We're in the twenty-first century, not the Victorian ages. Women may spend as much time working long hours and building careers as men do, so we're talking about making compromises and a bit of an effort to make sure we build a strong, solid relationship. There is so much fuss about what's expected from a man and what's expected from a woman that, instead of following our hearts, we try to copy others on what we think is best in a relationship. What works for one couple might not work for another. A relationship is a journey of discovery.

If you are with someone (woman or man), congratulations! Treat your partner with respect, and learn their likes and what's important to them. If you're single, congratulations! You are enjoying life and you are still finding out what it is that you truly want in your partner.

LADIES & GENTLEMEN

What we all must remember, both men and women, is that none of us is perfect. We need to learn to live with each other's "defects."

Relationships are not easy; there will be ups and there will be downs. But each step we take and each storm we go through is part of our learning process. Larry Wilson, author of *Play to Win*, describes it perfectly in one of his chapters. He says, "We learn and we grow from each failure."

Some of us are so scared of what might happen that we see any fight or failure as the end of the world. A war isn't won with just one battle. A war consists of many battles, and a relationship can be described pretty much like a war: to succeed in it, you'll go through some battles, but strength (or, in the case of relationships, love) will always prevail.

You can extend this analogy further. Dating is just a battle to be won before you can win the war. The ups and downs of engagement are a battle until you get married, thereby conquering the singles war.

Learning from different people is good for everyone. You can ask different couples what has worked for them and how they deal with difficulties. Wisdom doesn't come from just one person. Wisdom is collected throughout the years from the experience of many great minds. So don't be afraid to ask. Then figure out what works for you and your partner.

The difference between me and any other author or speaker out there is that we simply have different ways of explaining things, but the bottom line is that we all want people to become better at what they do and to achieve ultimate happiness and success. Always remember, your perfect match will be someone who pushes you to be the best you possibly can be in life.

RELATIONSHIPS IN GENERAL

Why do some people find it so hard to create long-lasting friendships? Why do so many friendships stop? One of the key elements mentioned before was honesty.

The U.S Marine Corp. is a great example to everybody. I have always admired their determination, courage, honesty, and loyalty. They use the Latin phrase *Semper Fi* to show camaraderie. It means "always faithful."

What if we applied that motto to our lives and the way we build relationships? Once again, it all comes down to our attitude. There is often too much jealousy among friends.

We've all heard people say some variation of, "Boyfriends and girlfriends come and go, but family and friends are for life." Well, unless we build on those relationships, they will not be there forever. Personal development is all about becoming a better human. So maybe you haven't been very good at making new friends or keeping them. That's not a problem! Make today the day you change your attitude and give relationships another go.

One of the greatest things about creating long-lasting friendships is that no matter the distance or how long it's been since you've last seen these people, when you next see them, it's as if no time has passed, and you simply pick up where you left off. I know that from personal experience. I have two amazing friends, Davy and Janet, whom I had not seen or spoken to for about a year, but when I finally caught up with them recently, it felt as if it was just yesterday that we last spoke. No matter where I am in the world, Davy and Janet will always be there as my friends. Still, we shouldn't let a whole year go by. Sometimes we get so caught up in our lives, struggles, or adversities that we stop talking to the people we should talk to the most. But that's the beauty of being a human being. We can all change our behavior, the way we think, and how we act and treat others.

Have you ever wondered why sometimes you meet someone and you just click? You know that you are going to be friends for life. Most of the time it's because that person thinks pretty much the same way you do. We tend to be attracted to such people, no matter what their background is. Think back to the different social groups when you were in school. Kids who listened to rock music stuck together, the math kids stuck together, the drama kids stuck together, the cheerleaders stuck together. They all behaved similarly to one another.

As we grow older, we expand our friends network because our minds develop. Maybe you were a cheerleader when you were younger, but are all your friends today only cheerleaders? Maybe you were one of the math kids, but are all your friends today computer technicians? Probably not.

When we were adolescents, we were divided according to the clothes we wore, the social group we belonged to, or the activities we did. Out of all the people you came in contact with as a kid, how many friendships have lasted until now? Most of us have a handful of people we are still friends with since we left school, but as we move on to bigger cities or different countries or change careers, our circle of friends changes and so do the relationships we create. This comes from being wiser and being able to judge people for who they are, not for the clothes they wear.

LETTING PEOPLE GO

One of the great things about being wiser is the ability to be able to drop some friendships. Yes, you heard me right—drop them!

Some relationships are harmful—they cause pain—and even though they hurt like a toothache, we keep them for fear of not gaining new friends. But to be able to move on, you sometimes have to let go. I've had to leave people behind, even when it was one of the hardest things I had ever had to do.

When you're trying to better yourself and achieve your goals and dreams, it is paramount to be surrounded by those who believe in you and won't put you down. I failed a few times in life because I let my so-called friends convince me I wasn't good enough, not realizing they were jealous and afraid I would become better than they were in their field of expertise. We all have mentors throughout life, whether they are teachers, friends, work colleagues, or family. It can be quite devastating when the people you look up to decide to turn against you and put you down because they see you as a threat. But once you understand why they are doing it, you become immune to their words and you simply let them go. You leave them behind.

And this is what having a Kick-Ass Attitude in relationships is all about. It's about learning to compromise, to let go of people who don't have the same vision as you and put you down instead of encouraging you.

Marcel Proust once said, "Let us be grateful to people who make us happy, they are the charming gardeners who make our souls blossom."

Relationships can be great when they are looked after, so cherish them and appreciate those who care for you.

4

YOUR DREAMS CAN COME TRUE

A TRIBUTE TO MICHAEL JACKSON, KING OF POP

I want to dedicate this chapter to Michael Jackson. This is my tribute to the legend and icon that he was, because he made dreams come true for not just himself, but for many others. He is a true example of what believing in yourself means.

Watching his memorial at the Staples Center in Los Angeles, I couldn't help but to shed tears. They were tears of both sadness and joy. Sadness because we had lost an icon, someone who made history around the world with his music and humanitarian efforts. And joy because his memorial was a celebration of what he had accomplished, all that he had achieved in his fifty years on this earth. It was a time of remembrance and a time to honor an incredible man who made an impact on many lives.

I will never forget Michael, as his song "Black and White" was the first song I learned in English when I was learning the language at the age of twelve back in Spain. I grew up listening and dancing to his music. He was also an inspiration because, through adversity and highs and lows in life, he never gave up. He kept on going and kept his dreams alive. I've always looked up to him as someone who, no matter what was going on, would always keep on going.

His memorial was full of friends and family speaking and telling stories about his life. Each and every one of them was full of heart and passion. What a way to commemorate his time on this earth. Each song performed brought tears to my eyes. It made me wonder, when it's my time to go, what will I be remembered for? I may not have millions of people watching my memorial, but I hope people see me as someone who followed her dreams and kept on going on matter what.

At the time of his death, Michael Jackson was ready for his comeback tour in London. One of his dreams was about to become reality when God said it was his time to go. God took him from his family, friends, and fans, but his legacy will live on. At the end of his memorial, when they sang "We Are the World" and "Heal the World," I got shivers all over, as the latter was one of his most precious songs and it reminded me that he created the Heal the World Foundation. He truly brought the world to a standstill on that day of his memorial service, July 7, 2009.

What we can take from Michael Jackson is the message to never stop following your dreams and, no matter what you do, work toward leaving a legacy in this world. As Michael would say:

> In a world filled with hate, we must still dare to hope. In a world filled with anger, we must still dare to comfort. In a world filled with despair, we must still dare to dream. And in a world filled with distrust, we must still dare to believe.

Farewell, Michael. We will never forget you.

LET'S GET STARTED

"Now, I say to you today my friends, even though we face the difficulties of today and tomorrow, I still have a dream. It is a dream deeply rooted in the American dream. I have a dream that one day this nation will rise up and live out the true meaning of its creed: "We hold these truths to be self-evident, that all men are created equal.""

–Martin Luther King Jr., speech during March on Washington, August 28, 1963

What an amazing passage! With those simple words, the truth is revealed. All men are created equal, and among them is the power to follow their dreams, to believe in them, and to act on them.

Why is it that so many people believe America to be the land of dreams? Such a new country and continent compared to Europe or Africa, yet it possesses the power of dreams. Let's take the Pledge of Allegiance as an example:

"I pledge allegiance to the flag

of the United States of America,

and to the republic for which it stands:

one nation under God, indivisible,

with liberty and justice for all."

A pledge that millions of people have recited with the purpose of following their dreams. Freedom! Shout many of them. Opportunity! Shout others. Whatever their reason, this pledge stands for not just the American dream, but for the dreams of anyone who believes in its meaning.

We hear stories from our ancestors that all start something like this:

"My grandmother came here with a dream of freedom and prosperity . . ."

"My dad brought me here with his last five bucks because he had a dream . . ."

"My family had this dream . . ."

What do they all have in common? Each of these people had a dream, a purpose, and a vision. Many ancestors sacrificed their lives and last cents to get to a place where dreams could become reality. They had passion, goals, and dreams that were not easily shattered. Their determination created the nation that we now know as the land of the free. But what has happened as the years have gone by? We forget what dreams are. We forget their true meaning.

The bottom line is, dreams are free. They don't cost a cent! They are part of who we are and can help us stay motivated to achieve our goals.

Now let's try to think about the last time we were actively dreaming. Get a piece of paper and write down three of your dreams, three of the things you want in life. They can be anything! Now read them out loud. I said out loud! OK, that's better. Didn't that make you smile? Dreams tend to put us in a happy state of mind. They make us smile because they're places where we can accomplish things that makes us happy.

Dreams can be anything you want them to be. Some people think dreams are those unreachable things that only the rich and famous can have. But let me tell you, money may buy you material possessions, but it will never buy your dreams. It will never buy the power of your mind and what you can achieve with it.

I'll share one of my dreams, and maybe some of you (especially the ladies) will understand me when I say that dreams can be anything. This may sound silly to a lot of people, but it took me years to find the perfect hairdresser. And when you finally find that one who makes your hair look like you belong in a shampoo commercial, you never go back to anyone else! I've been going to Barry for a few years now, and I will not allow anyone else to touch my hair. So I always tell him, the day I'm a millionaire I'll fly him to me when I need my hair done. Can you imagine? Being able to have that perfect haircut and style no matter where you are in the world just because you can?

So that is one of my goals, one of my dreams. It helps me focus to keep doing what I'm doing and never stop. The more dreams and goals you have, the more you will achieve in life. I said it earlier and I'll say it again; a failure is not a loss; it simply means you have to keep on trying. So train yourself to dream, to follow what you truly want. Like with anything else in life, you have to practice.

Pessimistic people always tell you that dreams are stupid, that there is no point in dreaming, that it's a waste of time and you should get real. Positive people, on the other hand, always tell you to keep dreaming, to dream big, and to never give up, because it's those who never give up who end up being winners. Remember that old saying, quitters never win and winners never quit. I totally agree with that. The people who put your dreams down are the ones who never followed theirs. They quit trying. But every time you talk to someone who has achieved what they want in life, they'll tell you to never quit, to follow your dreams no matter what.

Right now, as I'm writing this, I'm sitting in a coffee shop at Gatwick Airport. Earlier, sitting next to me, there was a father with four children, all very well behaved and happy. I spoke to him for a few minutes, as I noticed that he was watching his kids with a great smile while they were playing. There was something about him, the way he looked at his children, so I had to talk to him.

I found out that his wife had passed away a year ago and he was taking his children on a vacation in celebration of their mother's life. I felt compelled to find out more. I mean, most people would be sad and angry, but not this guy. He told me his wife had been ill for a while, so her passing was expected. His wife was a very positive and driven person and in her final months—she kept telling her husband to never stop dreaming and to give the children a life of belief, a life full of experiences, no matter what. Her passing should not be a sad time; she'd had a full life, and if God said it was her time to go, then it was her time to go.

He told me how she always enjoyed life and that he wanted his children to be the same. So this trip was a tribute to her and life. One of her dreams had been to vacation in a different country each year with the whole family, and her husband would keep that dream alive. Each year, he plans on taking the kids to a different location to experience new cultures, new friendships, and new horizons. His children, aged four, seven, twelve, and thirteen, all had this incredible air about them. I believe their mother's dreams will live on through them, and, in turn, they will create new dreams themselves, as they grow older.

Why did I share that story with you? Because it shows what the power of dreams is all about. Even after you are gone, you can leave a legacy to the people you care about and it doesn't cost you a cent. Be grateful for each day you have on this planet and let your dreams keep you going no matter what.

As I sit here at Gatwick, I see all these people waiting for family and friends to return from their flights. I see people hugging each other, people excited to see their loved ones. I see a grandmother in tears as she meets her grandchild and takes him into her arms for the first time.

No one can read minds, but we can read body language, and people with hopes and dreams show it in their faces. Right now, all the people I can see have that glow on their faces, a mixture of excitement and anxiety as they wait for people they may have not seen in a very long time. At this moment, their dream is to see that person, and their faces light up when they do.

I said it already, and I'll mention it again: a dream is whatever you want it to be. It can be quite overwhelming sometimes. Our minds are limitless, so take advantage of it! Follow your dreams. There is nothing you cannot do. We just need a little bit of magic when it comes to creating dreams. And by magic, I mean attitude and belief.

We always hear, "I'm not a kid anymore; I have to grow up." We get caught up in the little things in life that won't matter a year from today and we forget to pursue what we truly want. One way of pursuing what you want is to create your list of goals. Write them on a piece of paper and have them visible, so each day you are reminded of them.

Another way of doing it—and this is my favorite—is to create a vision board. Many people have used this concept in many fields, but the person I learned it from was my mentor, Lisa. For those of you who don't know what a vision board is, it's a board where you put pictures of things you want in life or words that encourage you. A vision board can contain anything—a photo of your dream home; your dream holiday; your perfect body; the car you've always dreamed of; or words to inspire you like "success," "courage," and "never give up."

This board is to be filled with your dreams so they can

become reality. The more you look at something you want, the harder you will work to get it. You need to have that "why," that goal, and that vision to achieve it!

Because you can't walk around each day with a huge board, create a mini version of it, with three of the things that you want the most. Then put it in your car's sun visor, or carry it with you in a bag. Put it somewhere you will see it every day when you are out and about.

It's surprising how many people don't have a list of goals or a vision board. Then they wonder why they get derailed from following what they want in life.

Not everyone wants to dream big, and that's OK. I talk to many people who, when asked what their dreams are, are so taken aback by what's going on in their lives right now that they can't concentrate on dreaming big. Some people answer, "What's the point of dreaming? I'm never going to get it." That's where creating a Kick-Ass Attitude comes in! You need to have the attitude first to be able to believe, to believe in something bigger than yourself.

Having a vision, having a dream, has driven many

successful people to where they are today. They didn't let their circumstances get in the way. Some of us will get there quicker than others, but no matter how long it takes us, it is the passion for and belief in what we want that will take us to our final destination.

I have always dreamed a lot, probably too much. My mom would always tell me I was a dreamer and that I was always on cloud nine. I guess I was a bit of a rebel, as I didn't listen to what she said and I kept on dreaming.

Don't allow other people to interfere when it comes to following what you want in life. From personal experience, I can tell you it takes a lot of willpower to not allow others to influence what you do. I allowed that many years ago, and it derailed me from my path. Do I regret it? Yes and no. Never regret anything you have done in life, as it is all part of your life experience. We may not make the wisest decisions all the time, but we learn from each mistake. The bigger the dreams, the more you will keep to your path.

As George Bernard Shaw once said: "You see things, and you say, 'Why?' But I dream things that never were, and I say, 'Why not?'"

So keep your dreams alive and never give up!

5

SELF BELIEF & MINDSET

How many times do we stop following our dreams because we think we aren't good enough?

When people don't succeed in life, one of the main reasons is that they don't have enough SELF-BELIEF. We have to learn to believe more in ourselves and we have to give ourselves more credit than we do. We might be great at encouraging other people, but we can't seem to apply the same advice to ourselves.

Our brains are complex organs—they are in constant use, always thinking, always doing something, even when we are asleep. Training our brains is not an easy task, but we can all become better at it.

Many times throughout life we have wanted to do things, but our inner voice keeps saying, "What if it doesn't work? Are you really good enough? Are you sure you can do it? Who are you to do it? You don't have enough experience!"

Do those words sound familiar? This inner fear and self-doubt cause us a lot of pain in life. We have to start believing in ourselves more. We hear people say, "You have to believe it to achieve it," and I totally agree with that. Before anything can be achieved, before you can accomplish anything in life, you have to believe you are capable of achieving anything you want.

We ask ourselves, "How am I going to do it, how am I going to achieve it?" The answer is, you must always have faith in who you are and what you can achieve. The power of self-belief lies within our hearts, within ourselves. When we truly believe in our own abilities, there is very little that we can't achieve. So we have to determine what our abilities are and make them stronger.

DIFFERENT TYPES OF MINDSETS

To be able to believe in ourselves and our goals, we must have the correct mindset. Believe me, you don't get one without the other. Our mindset creates our whole mental world. It shapes our goals and our attitude toward work and relationships, and it ultimately predicts whether we will fulfill our potential.

According to more than thirty-five years of research conducted by Professor Carol Dweck of Napier University, it can be concluded that everyone has one of two basic mindsets: fixed mindset and growth mindset. The following is from Dweck's 2006 book, *Mindset: The new psychology of success.*

> In a "growth" mindset, people believe that their most basic qualities can continually be enhanced and developed with effort and practice. As a consequence, they actively enjoy opportunities to learn and improve—to become more competent— even at the risk of appearing to others as less than perfect at something. The confidence levels of "growth" mindset individuals are therefore robust as people in this mindset appreciate learning from failure and seek further learning to remedy any perceived deficits.

> In a "fixed" mindset, however, people believe that their basic qualities are basically carved in stone and that mistakes mean these qualities are somehow inadequate. They believe that their reputations and sense of self rest on appearing flawless to other people. Professor Carol Dweck discovered that people with a "fixed" mindset often avoided opportunities to improve their skills and

abilities, because (a) they didn't expect effort would make any difference and (b) that having to put effort into something only proved that they weren't good at it in the first place. Self-confidence in this mindset is fragile and requires constant success and praise to maintain it.

It is possible to have a fixed mindset in one area of your life (for example, your attitude to how good at sports you are) and a growth mindset in another area (for example, your attitude to learning languages). However, research also shows that developing a "growth" mindset overall is much more likely to lead to success in life. For example, research with university students found that "growth" mindset students achieved significantly better grades than "fixed" mindset students regardless of how they scored in measures of intelligence. In other words, mindset was the better predictor of success. Intelligence is not fixed but grows with effort and practice.

And the Good News is...it is never too late to modify a mindset because the brain is a muscle, which improves with exercise! How you interpret challenges, setbacks, and criticism is your choice. You can interpret them in a fixed mindset as signs that your fixed talents or abilities are lacking. Or you can interpret them in a growth mindset as signs that you need to ramp up your strategies and effort, stretch yourself, and expand your abilities. It's up to you.

Now you should have a better understanding as to why mindset plays such a paramount part in your self-belief. No matter what task you are about to endure, mindset is the prep work you need before achieving anything. Let's take athletes and Olympians as an example. What do you think goes through their minds before any event? If you pay attention, you'll see they are focused—sometimes they close their eyes. No matter what is around them, their mindset is on what's going to happen. They have a positive and growth mindset telling them they can do it. This is their event, they are the best, they have trained for this, they know they can do it, and they give themselves positive affirmations. That mindset helps them create the self-belief they need to go for it whether they win or lose. They create that Kick-Ass Attitude to know they are going to do their best no matter what.

SALES PEOPLE

How about door-to-door sales people? I truly admire them. Their mindset is incredibly strong. Most people don't like when a sales rep knocks on their door as they are having dinner or are in the middle of something. Can you imagine what these people go through? People slamming doors on them and being rude, knocking after knocking after knocking. But it's the job they have chosen for now, so their mindset prepares them for the tasks ahead. They know they are going to be shouted at and have doors shut in their faces, but they think, "Someone out there will listen" and "Each slamming door is a step closer to someone keeping the door open." It is their mindset that gets them going before they go out on the road.

And how about our favorite people, telemarketers? They seem to have the best timing in the world. They always call when you are in the middle of taking a shower, watching your favorite TV show, or enjoying a meal. Whether we like it or not, it is another job that people do. It pays their bills and puts food on their tables and clothes on their bodies. So even though telemarketers are some of the least liked people around the world, they do have a strong mindset. Just like door-to-door salespeople, they create that growth mindset and believe that each phone being hung up is a step closer to someone listening.

Now, I don't have anything against door-to-door sales people or telemarketers. One of the reasons I chose those two as examples is that throughout my life I have had the experience of doing both! And I know how you feel when someone closes the door or hangs up the phone on you.

I remember when I was sixteen and I got my first job. It was door-to-door sales. Imagine that—a young lady just turned sixteen going door to door, both residential and commercial, trying to sell stuff for a few bucks. It was daunting, it was scary, and my mom thought I was nuts! But I worked on commission, and the reward of seeing some cash after selling something was worth it. It wasn't the money itself; it was knowing that with persistence and belief, anything is possible. That some people would say yes even though hundreds wouldn't even listen. Did I get it right the first time? Of course not. Did I end up crying at the beginning because people weren't giving me a chance? Of course I did. That is where my Kick-Ass Attitude started, and I even didn't know it. I didn't allow anyone to beat me! I had goals! I wanted to do things with the extra cash, and I was not going to let a few slammed doors get in the way of what I wanted. It was then that I learned persistence pays off and that it all starts with your mindset.

Then, about two years later, when I was in the UK and got my first real job as a trainee photographer, I endured the experience of telemarketing. Part of my training was to call leads—people who had expressed interest in having their photos taken. What a challenge that was! Number one, English was my second language and it wasn't as good as it is now, and number two, I had never done it before. But I approached it the same way as I had approached my door-to-door sales experience. The more people you called, the more people who would say yes. It all came down to my mindset before I picked up that phone.

So, what resonates throughout this chapter is that mindset, self-belief and attitude all go together. It's a chain reaction.

Think back and look at all the things you have done in life since you were a kid, and you will discover how many times your mindset and self-belief got you through it without you even realizing it. It sure makes me smile when I look back! As I said in chapter 1, when we were kids, we had the best mindset ever. Nothing could get in our way. So remember that feeling and use it to inspire you to have a growth mindset.

Realizing the power of your true self is one of the most important realizations you will ever make. And one of the hardest, too. But it's this journey of self-discovery that will make you into the person you want to be. We already know that no two people are alike and that not everyone moves at the same pace so look at each step forward as a step closer to finding who you truly are. Find the inner god or goddess who can achieve anything in life.

In the words of Zig Ziglar: "If you want to reach a goal, you must 'see the reaching' in your own mind before you actually arrive at your goal."

E. Carolina Quevedo

6

BUSINESS LEGENDS & SUCCESS STORIES
-They all have a Kick-Ass Attitude-

With the right attitude, many people achieve success. But what is success? Does it mean the same thing to everyone? According to WordNet, success may mean:

1. An event that accomplishes its intended purpose; "let's call heads a success and tails a failure"; "the election was a remarkable success for Republicans."

2. An attainment that is successful; "his success in the marathon was unexpected"; "his new play was a great success."

3. A state of prosperity or fame; "he is enjoying great success"; "he does not consider wealth synonymous with success."

4. A person with a record of successes; "his son would never be the achiever that his father was"; "only winners need apply"; "if you want to be a success you have to dress like a success."

Source: WordNet 1.7.1 Copyright © 2001 by Princeton University.

In this chapter we are going to see different levels of success as we go through some business legends, and we will see how their Kick-Ass Attitudes got them to where they are today. Don't feel pressured to be exactly like them; take their determination, passion for what they do, and attitude as a starting point. We all need role models to look up to, but that doesn't mean we must achieve the same goals as they did.

We need to start by studying the successful people we look up to, learn what they do, and then simply adapt it to suit our needs. Tony Robbins says, "Modeling is the pathway to excellence," which means it's OK to model someone to start with, but eventually we have to develop into our own person. We have to take risks and take the leap toward creating our own philosophy.

This is where a Kick-Ass Attitude plays a big part. Copying someone is safe. Attending seminars without taking action is safe. But creating your own ideas and implementing them can be quite daunting and not safe at all. Failure is part of the learning curve, as we have seen throughout the chapters, and by having the right attitude and knowing success is there for the taking, creating our own ideas and stepping out of our comfort zone becomes not so daunting after all!

This chapter is all about realizing that even the biggest business legends or successful people need to have the right attitude. We all relate to different people's stories, so I chose a variety of men and women who I believe everyone around the world can relate to, no matter where you are in life right now.

I have met some of them through my travels, and others are people I simply admire and respect because of what they have accomplished. Those are the ones I call "business legends." Some of the names will be familiar; others won't be. Don't look at their fame—instead look carefully at what has made them succeed regardless of what industry they are in.

They are all great leaders in their fields, and if you can relate to any of them and want to share your story, email me at info@elisequevedo.com. Hearing your stories is one of my best rewards; so don't be afraid to contact me!

BUSINESS LEGENDS

BILL G: chairman of Microsoft (co-founder with Paul Allen), American business magnate and philanthropist

Gates is one of the world's wealthiest people and is one of the best-known entrepreneurs in the field of computers. While growing up in Seattle, he discovered his interest in software and computer programming at age thirteen. No one knew what a legend he would become. He and his wife created the Bill and Melinda Gates Foundation, which work to increase access to innovations in education, technology, and world health. It shows that being a business legend isn't all about making money, but also giving back.

"As we look ahead into the next century, leaders will be those who empower others," Gates once said. "As I look forward, I'm very optimistic about the things I see ahead."

Gates never concentrated on what went wrong in his life. He knew he would ultimately succeed no matter how many times he failed, and that's called a Kick-Ass Attitude. His first company, Traf-O-Data, flopped, but he kept going and worked harder to make his future ventures work. A few decades ago, the home computer or microchip seemed like something from *Star Trek* or *Back to the Future*. Nowadays, if you don't own a computer and cell phone, people think you belong in the Dark Ages. Gates saw the potential in the market and never gave up. Bill Gates is and always will be a business legend.

ABRAHAM L: sixteenth president of the United States

Let's take a look at Lincoln's road to presidency. It all came down to his attitude to keep himself going.

It took him nearly thirty years to become president of the United States. Between 1830 and 1860, the year he was elected, Lincoln suffered a nervous breakdown; was defeated several times for election to the Senate, House of Representatives, and vice presidency; and he also failed in business. But he never gave up. He also suffered from dyslexia, making him an inspiration to anyone with a learning disability. Lincoln's story is proof that you can achieve anything you want in life. To this day, Lincoln remains one of the greatest presidents in U.S. history. He also possessed the classical values of honesty and integrity, and his legacy lives on because of it. Do you have the Kick-Ass Attitude to keep going no matter how many years it takes to get to your final destination?

> "There are no accidents in my philosophy. Every effect must have its cause. The past is the cause of the present, and the present will be the cause of the future. All these are links in the endless chain stretching from the finite to the infinite."
>
> "Leave nothing for tomorrow which can be done today."

– Abraham Lincoln

DONALD T: American business legend, author, television personality, and chairman of the Trump Organization

Trump has a flare for spotting good deals, and he doesn't let anyone get in his way of achieving his dreams. On my way back from a conference in Toronto a couple of years ago, I bought one of his books, *Think Big and Kick Ass in Business and Life*, co-written with Bill Zanker. I couldn't put it down. Trump is so direct and to the point.

Trump began his career in real estate by working for his father. Soon after that he moved to Manhattan, where he started his path to fame. Even though he went through a lot of financial problems in the late 80s and 90s, he turned everything around to become the household name that we know today.

Not only has he made it big in the real estate business, but he's also become a highly paid TV personality thanks to the reality show *The Apprentice*. He's no fool when it comes to making the most out of each situation. He sees opportunities and grabs them. He went from being paid $50,000 per episode to over $3 million at one point. And because of *The Apprentice*, he now has his own star on the Hollywood Walk of Fame.

Something I have learned from "The Donald" (the nickname given to him by his ex-wife Ivana) is to follow your gut instinct. Read some of his books or watch some of his interviews and you'll notice he talks about following your gut feeling. He tells you to think of what you want, not what others want you to do or think. Trump didn't get where he is today by following everyone else. He created his own path and led himself to victory.

SIR RICHARD B: English entrepreneur and founder of Virgin Atlantic (among many others)

Who doesn't know whom this man is?! He has been a success story since the age of sixteen, when he created *Student* magazine. In the 70s he opened Virgin Records stores, which eventually became Virgin Megastores, and he came a worldwide business icon thanks to Virgin Atlantic airways. *Forbes* listed Branson among the three hundred richest people in the world in 2009.

It may come as a surprise to some people that when Richard Branson was a kid he suffered from dyslexia and was a poor student. His attitude made him succeed and find excellence in other areas of life, like playing sports and connecting with people.

Sir Richard Branson (he was knighted in 1999) has received many awards, but the one I admire him for the most is his 2007 United Nations Correspondents Association Citizen of the World Award. Like Bill Gates, Branson supports many humanitarian causes. He gives back to the people who need it.

What we can take from Branson is his determination and passion for what he believes in. The Virgin Empire shows no signs of slowing down and his legacy will continue for centuries to come.

SUCCESS STORIES –

Success stories do not always have to be told by famous people. Sometimes it is the everyday person who can be a success story and who can inspire us all. And for this reason I am starting with my great friend Debi.

Debi Kieserman – Mom, businesswoman, entrepreneur.

I met my friend Debi on a cruise in October 2008 and we instantly became close friends. It's one of those unexplainable things, we just clicked; we "got" each other. No judgments, more like support and unending encouragement for each other's hopes and dreams. Debi was born and raised in the suburbs of Philadelphia, attended college at The George Washington University in Washington, D.C. A few years after she graduated, she got married and moved to southern Florida where they raised her two daughters. In Florida she built from scratch an event production business creating marvelous parties for the Florida elite. She produced events for President Clinton, Steve Forbes as well as the World Series events for the Florida Marlins baseball team. She became the breadwinner for her family earning an impeccable reputation based on integrity and creativity.

Fast forward 20 years to the present, we find Debi single, and yearning for adventure. Her daughters are now in school, the youngest in college and the oldest daughter in medical school. She decided to sell her home, sell her business and start "chapter two" of her life in Los Angeles.

During my recent visit to LA, Debi and I shared much laughter sandwiched between intense talks about our lives, our goals and the obstacles that stand before us. With each other's help, we designed strategies to accomplish our dreams

For me, Debi is an inspiration. It proofs that no matter what stage you are at in life, it is never too late to follow your dreams.

LISA J: best-selling author, coach and international speaker

I first met Lisa in February 2007 in Phoenix. Like anyone who has attended one of her trainings, I was blown away. I knew I had to know more about this powerful woman. At that time, I knew one day she would be my mentor. And that happened within twelve months of my meeting her.

What made this woman stand out from the rest? What made her succeed? She is the ultimate role model, not just in business, but at home too. She is a powerful businesswoman and a mother of three wonderful children. Lisa reaches out to people by talking about how she broke through self-limiting beliefs to achieve success. She teaches you how to be bold and conquer your fears.

She is a great example of how being a mom is no excuse to not succeed in business.

I love her boldness, and it comes as no surprise that her events sell out and her books are sold all over the world. Her laughter is contagious and her generosity is beyond imagination.

Her success is a combination of personal past experiences and personal growth and development.

Lisa is an inspiration to any mom out there who thinks she can't do it all. Balance is the key for Lisa. She knows when to be a mom, when to be a coach, and when to be the woman she truly is.

JULIAN METCALFE: co-founder of Prêt A Manger

I had the pleasure of interviewing Julian earlier this year. People who create successful businesses based on true passion for their fields always intrigue me. Prêt A Manger is a chain of sandwich shops in the UK, New York, and Hong Kong.

Julian had a passion for food and decided he wanted to create a place where the food was better than the rest. A lot of people want to have their own business or dream about doing something they've never done before, but they never do it because the people around them shatter those dreams. I asked Julian if he ever had people around him telling him it would never work. And if so, what kept him going? What made him keep believing what he was doing was the right thing? He said he knew if he asked too many people, he wouldn't do it. So even though you need to listen to people's advice, sometimes it's better if you don't and simply trust your instinct.

Julian is a perfectionist. He has a great attention for detail and is never complacent. He cares today as much as he cared the first day he started in business. What does success mean to Julian? Realizing his goals, being content, and making sure his family and other people alongside him are happy. He believes harmony around him is key. I asked him what would he tell anyone who is after success or has a dream but isn't sure they can go out and do it, someone who wants to be a leader in life, not a follower. Julian believes you need to have a passion for what you are doing. You must have a high level of determination, be very tenacious, and stick to what you are doing. Believe in yourself and never give up. Pursue perfection.

MICHAEL P: most successful Olympian ever

And what a success story this is. At twenty-four years of age, Michael has won fourteen Olympic gold medals, the most by any Olympian in history, and he has also set thirty-seven world records in swimming. His performance at the 2008 Beijing Olympics stunned viewers around the world.

This is what attitude, determination, and hard work are all about. Phelps didn't just win all these medals by luck. Years of training were behind the success he has created. Training is a discipline and, like anything else, must be nurtured and matured. His concentration prior to any of his performances was beyond anything I have ever seen. It was just him and the water.

Apply his attitude to any sport you wish to take on, and you'll succeed.

STORIES

How many stories do you have to share with the people around you? What stories will be told about you in the years to come?

Success stories and business legends aren't born overnight. They are developed and worked on for many years, and each and every one of us can be one of them.

Each new day brings us the opportunity to become better, to create a better attitude and to develop ourselves into powerful and successful human beings.

I have many stories left to tell that I will share in due course. From each experience we go through we learn something, and, whether it's good or bad, it's part of who we are today. Learning to let go and learning new ways of thinking are not easy! But it's a simple concept. Who we are today is due to the way we have been thinking and behaving for many years. If we want to change and improve our lifestyle, we need to be open minded, have the right attitude, and keep our eyes open to the world to personal development.

We are all worthy individuals, and to sum it up in one word, we are simply . . . AWESOME!

E. Carolina Quevedo

7

CREATING A KICK-ASS ATTITUDE IN YOUR MIND

As I thought the book was finished, I decided to add one more chapter. A final step onto the way I think, the way I see motivation, the way I would like to see people think a bit more. Hence 'Creating a Kick-Ass Attitude" in your mind.

There is no editing on this chapter, no revising, no second guesses, no looking back, no take backs.

This is all about me writing with the flow, writing at home listening to some chill out music whilst I let inspiration, my heart and mind tell me what to write. Sometimes people ask me how did you start a chapter? how did you start your book? How did you manage to accomplish it?

The simple answer to all those questions is... you just get on with it and do it. It is that first word that normally is the hardest, but once you start typing, one word seems to follow the next. It is hard to explain. All I know is that we all have a book within us, and we can all start typing. Life is like a blank storybook. What happens in the next chapter is up to us. We all choose what action comes next. What do you want your storybook to say? What is the next chapter in your life? We have spoken about this during this book; it all starts with our attitude. With the desire to do something. Our mind is more powerful than we think and we seem to doubt it more that we should!

As I write this I seem to have a big smile on my face, listening to some instrumental music and just typing away. It gives me great pleasure to know that someone one day will be reading this book and will think of doing the same.

There is one thing I always say: "Always go to bed with a smile on your face". I know it's easier said than done, but smiling seems to always put my mind at ease. Making things clearer. I have a very good friend of mine, (who I'll name Barnie to keep the identity a mystery), and my little reminder every night is to make sure he smiles before he goes to bed. I think he got a bit fed up when I originally started asking him if he had remembered to smile!! Ha ha!! But now is a habit! And a good habit that puts your mind at ease and makes you realize that life no matter how many challenges brings is not as hard as we think.

In life we need to break down challenges into small stages to be able to accomplish them.

Some of you might say, " Oh its easy for her to say that!" or " yeah right, you are not in my situation".

Well trust me, I have been at the bottom; I have been on top, then at bottom again, then on the rise like a Phoenix rising from the ashes. I know exactly how you might feel. There have been occasions when as an example, when writing this book I wanted to throw the towel, or I simply thought I wasn't good enough. That nobody would be interested in reading what I had to say. But you know what? I looked at myself in the mirror and realized that only I was thinking that, no one was telling me not to do it or that I wasn't good enough. We are the ones that sabotage ourselves when it comes to accomplishing what we want to achieve in life.

"Creating a Kick-Ass Attitude" in the mind, means motivating yourself, looking in the mirror each day and saying " what am I going to accomplish today?" "What am I going to conquer?" "Who am I going to inspire?" " Who will I make proud today?"

We each have our own reasons as to why we want to succeed, why we want to leave a legacy and why we want to make a name for ourselves. Whatever those reasons are, never forget them. Write them down and remember them each day.

My mind sometimes has so many thoughts that is hard to make sense of any of it, but you know what? I love it!!!!

It's called being a dreamer and wanting to achieve anything you want in life.

I believe we all have the potential to be great beings in this earth. From the day we were born, a life was given to us full of possibilities, full of opportunities. What you do with them is up to you. They say opportunities don't knock very often; well guess what! Make your own! We make our own opportunities!! Life is full of them! You just need to open your eyes and mind and be ready to step and think outside box. And after you start to see it, start acting on it!

Too many people talk, talk, talk, but not many act, act, act. As they say " actions speak louder than words".

Amazing what pops into our minds; just now I'm thinking how many of my "so called" friends will actually buy a copy of this book. I've had many people anticipating the launch of it to buy it, but I guarantee that not even half of them will go get a copy. Why? Because people talk to the talk but don't walk the walk. We must always remember, not everyone is passionate about the same subjects as we are. And that is ok! I don't even know why I shared that, but as I said at the beginning of this chapter, this is all about writing from inspiration, with no looking back or re-editing what I've typed or deleting something that may not make any sense!

And this is exactly what makes me, ME! I am unique, I have my own style and you either like it or not. It's called freedom of speech and it's what makes this world great!

I truly hope this can inspire everyone out there to be better in life, to believe that you can achieve what you want in life and to help others achieve what they want.

But how do you get motivated to do anything? How do you take that first step? How do you balance work, family and life in general?! By simply taking one step at a time.

The saying " A journey of a thousand miles begins with a first step" is one of the most powerful sayings in my mind. The Same as " Rome was not built in a day".

Sometimes we try to jump steps then we fall flat and we don't know how to get up. Falling is never a problem, as long as we are doing it one step at a time.

Ask any successful person if they ever fell on their journey and they will probably say. " You have no idea how many times!" As that is part of the journey of success; falling, failing and learning from what went wrong. It's what makes our character stronger.

Everything being said right now is a reiteration of everything said in the book, a reminder, call it a compilation if you wish, in plain simple English.

My mind likes to wonder a lot, it is what I like to call my own motivation. I imagine what things will look like in the future. I imagine speaking in front of bigger audiences than I have before. I imagine how successful my 5th or 6th book will be! I imagine what my next vacation will be like. I imagine how many countries I will have houses in so I can travel in between them anytime I want, I imagine the cars I have not yet driven, etc.

Now do you see what my mind is doing here? My mind is keeping my motivation alive! They both work together so that each time I get derailed or I have doubts, I think of all the things that are coming my way. All the possibilities and all the opportunities I have not yet seen and achieved!

In essence, it is our goals that keep us going. Most successful people have a huge list of goals and dreams and to do lists, and those who never accomplish anything, don't even understand what goals are.

Sometimes I am surprised at how many people do not have a list or don't even think of dreams because they don't see a point on it. It's what separates us from the rest. We are always striving to do better and to achieve more.

Now something important here, remember to share your goals and dreams with the people you love and care about. There is only so much one person can accomplish. I used to think I could do everything alone, that I was enough and that I knew everything in life! Boy was I wrong! Although no one will walk our walk, and no one will live our lives, accomplishing your goals is a lot easier when people who believe in what you do surround you. People who remind you to keep focused, people who push you to be the best you possibly can be. And people who are there for you when you feel like throwing in the towel.

Trust me, I have been there and it's a lot easier when you are surrounded by people who think the same way as you do. We spoke about it in the Relationships chapter, so read back if you forgot what I'm talking about!

Now, I don't want to rumble too much on this chapter. All good things have to come to an end! Haha

But keep on reading, there are still a couple of pages left before we bid farewell.

Gosh, farewell? Now I sound like I'm on the 1800's!! I have been known to make cheesy quotes from the olden days once in a while, but as I always say… you either like it or not! And in my world, I'm always right! Haha

There are a couple more things I would like to share with you or remind you of.

Whatever it is that you want to accomplish, do it all with honesty and integrity. Those are two of my favorite traits in people. I value, respect and admire people who posses those qualities.

And whatever you do, do it with passion. I have met a few people in life who are soooooo passionate about what they do, that I'm always at awe when I meet them and hear them talk about what they do or where they are going.

Let me give you an example; I still remember the first time I met my very good friend Alex (although I have lots of friends called Alex, you know who you are after reading this!!!! hehe) and we sat down talking about where we were going in life. We sat down for hours talking and inspiring each other. It had been a while since I had met someone so fiery, full of ideas and full of life. I remember going home with a huge grin on my face, I couldn't stop thinking about the mind-blowing session I had just had with someone who basically was a stranger!! Then again in the personal development world this is not uncommon! Alex is now someone who I care about very much and a very close friend of mine. This little mention is my thank you to you Alex, and a reminder that I cannot wait to see you at the top!!! The passion you have for what you believe in is an inspiration and I know you will be leaving a legacy for future generations. You know I'm behind you 100%, love you and I'm proud of everything you are doing and I love our mind blowing sessions!! Ha-ha Boom Zoom all the way right?! (Guys you'll have to wait for the next book to find out what the Boom Zoom is, as only 3 people know!! haha)

In life we all have friends who inspire us and who we inspire. I look forward to writing my next book so I can share more stories about my great friends and how they inspire me. Although, I do want to make a mention to my friend Alison. I have known you for over 13 years and no matter where we have ended up in the world, our friendship has remained strong and pure. You have been there in the great times and the hard times. Thank you for being you. Plenty of stories out there from all the places we have been to! But I guess I will wait for the next book, I may even share our Disneyland story where you fell flat in your butt at the Buffalo Bill show. Remember that?! I still cannot think about it without laughing! What a trip that was! And this just takes us back to what I was saying before in regards smiling. We all have memories and stories that will always make us giggle. When you are having a not so good day, pop one of those memories in your mind and relive those happy times for there are plenty more to come in the future.

If you look closely, inspiration can be found in the little things or actions people do. So pay attention at what people do for you. Buying you a drink, giving you a lift home, bailing you out when you are in trouble. Or simply listening to you vent when you are having a bad day. And trust me, we have all had those!! We just don't seem to think about it.

Right guys, this chapter is coming to an end, which means this book is officially finished!

Wow! I cannot believe I officially said that, this book is officially finished. Maybe I should include a picture of me with a huge grin on my face! It has been a long journey, but worth it all the way.

All good things must come to and end for new ones to start!

So that's it folks! It's been a pleasure sharing my thoughts and stories with you.

Until next time, farewell my dear friends....

Have an awesome day!!

8

FINAL THOUGHTS

-TOP TEN TIPS TO CREATE A KICK-ASS

ATTITUDE-

1. Think more like a child once in a while. Remember how fearless you were as a kid and you will start taking more chances when it comes to following your goals.

2. Change the attitude you have toward your job, and always remember that no matter what it is you're doing right now, it's all part of your journey and not your destination.

3. Take each fall or failure you go through as a learning experience that will make you grow stronger.

4. In any type of relationship, always remember *Semper Fi*. Loyalty, honesty and integrity are what build all relationships.

5. Allow yourself to believe your dreams CAN come true. Repeat it over and over again in your mind.

6. Create a vision board full of all the things you want to achieve in life. Visualization will help you keep focus.

7. Train yourself to dream, to follow what you truly want. It's like anything else in life—you have to practice!

8. When you wake up each morning, smile and remind yourself YOU are worthy of everything that is coming your way. Hard work always pays off.

9. Believe in yourself and concentrate on what YOU want to become.

10. CREATE A KICK-ASS ATTITUDE IN EVERY ASPECT OF LIFE!!!!!!!!!!

To your success,

Elise Carolina Quevedo

www.elisequevedo.com

YOUR 100 LIST OF GOALS & DREAMS

1. _____

2. _____

3. _____

4. _____

5. _____

6. _____

7. _____

8. _____

9. _____

10. _____

11. _____

12. _____

13. _____

14. _____

15. _____

16. _____

17. _____

18. _____

19. _____

20. _____

21. _____

22. _____

23. _____

24. _____

25. _____

26. _____

27. _____

28. _____

29. _____

30. _____

31. _____

32. _____

33. _____

34. _____

35. _____

36. _____

37. _____

38. _____

39. _____

40. _____

41. _____

42. _____

43. _____

44. _____

45. _____

46. _____

47. _____

48. _____

49. _____

50. _____

51. _____

52. _____

53. _____

54. _____

55. _____

56. _____

57. _____

58. _____

59. _____

60. _____

61. _____

62. _____

63. _____

64. _____

65. _____

66. _____

67. _____

68. _____

69. _____

70. _____

71. _____

72. _____

73. _____

74. _____

75. _____

76. _____

77. _____

78. _____

79. _____

80. _____

81. _____

82. _____

83. _____

84. _____

85. _____

86. _____

87. _____

88. _____

89. _____

90. _____

91. _____

92. _____

93. _____

94. _____

95. _____

96. _____

97. _____

98. _____

99. _____

100.   _____

YOUR MANTRA LIST

Hey guys, remember we spoke about mantras and the importance in having certain phrases/sentences that can help you during the week? I want you to create your own list. Write them down and live by them!

1. _i.e. " Anything is possible" _____

2. _i.e. "I am worth it" _____

3. _i.e. " I can do anything I set my mind to" _____

4. _____

5. _____

6. _____

7. _____

8. _____

9. _____

10. _____

11. _____

12. _____

13. _____

14. _____

15. _____

16. _____

17. _____

18. _____

19. _____

20. _____

21. _____

22. _____

23. _____

24. _____

25. _____

26. _____

27. _____

28. _____

SOME OF MY FAVOURITE QUOTES

Please note, the quotes below are on public domain. Thank you.

- "When love and skill work together, expect a masterpiece" by John Ruskin

- "Use what talents you posses: the woods would be very silent if no birds sang there except those that sang best" by Henry Van Dyke

- " To accomplish great things, we must not only act, but also dream; not only plan, but also believe" by Anatole France

- " Those who act receive the prizes" by Aristotle

- "Keep away from people who try to belittle your ambitions. Small people always do that, but the really great make you feel that you, too, can become great" by Mark Twain

- "If you don't have a goal or plan of where you want to go in life, you usually don't like where you end up" by E. Carolina Quevedo

- " You have to learn the rules of the game. And then you have to play better than anyone else" by Albert Einstein

- "Moderation is a fatal thing. Nothing succeeds like excess" by Oscar Wilde

- "Great works are performed not by strength, but by perseverance" by Samuel Johnson

- " When the student is ready, the master appears" Buddhist Proverb

- "In any moment of decision the best thing you can do is the right thing, the next best thing is the wrong thing, and the worst thing you can do is nothing" by Theodore Roosevelt

- "It is quality rather than quantity that counts" by Seneca

- " Pleasure and action make the hours seem short" by William Shakespeare

- "Losers never win and winners never quit" by Anonymous

E. Carolina Quevedo

Made in the USA
Charleston, SC
09 February 2012